"America, America!"

A Letter to the Nation
Written as a Collection of Poetry

by

Hon. Torrance R. Harvey Sr.

DORRANCE
PUBLISHING CO
EST. 1920
PITTSBURGH, PENNSYLVANIA 15238

Dorrance Publishing Co
585 Alpha Drive
Suite 103
Pittsburgh, PA 15238
Visit our website at *www.dorrancebookstore.com*

ISBN: 978-1-6366-1552-3
eISBN: 978-1-6366-1716-9

"America, America!"

America, America
(Inspired by James Baldwin)
October 31st, 2020

America, America, land of the free
and home of the brave

Land of our forefathers for which you never saved on the
forefront of American prosperity when America never wanted
me and my ancestors to be truly free

Because my ancestors were enslaved
Not even for how he or she behaved

The U.S. Constitution said we were made as 3/5th of a human
to count your population count for that bicameral legislature
HAD to be made

Oh, America, America, land of the free
Home of the brave

The non-free black man was skilled yet killed & the dry bones
remain still in his tragic grave

Medgar, Martin, and Malcolm

Tragically torn from society but more importantly torn from
their own beloved families

Their daughters of the night, still weep at night as their torn
souls sleep and their mamas still wept themselves to sleep
many nights

No matter what I do I'm still crazy over you, America

But there are things we all still dread

you don't seem to care about the children whose famous
fathers are now dead

North, South, East, West

If you are a black man or a colored immigrant
You're a second-class citizen reduced to nothing again and again

America, America

Tell Mr. Charlie to leave me alone

Your ideology of purity rejects but needs to reflect back to
ancient dry bones

Check your blood blueprint

Check your polypeptide stands

We are all made from the same human

Then observe and trace the lifelines in the palms of your hands

You part negro too

The story of the negro is the story of America
for which you already scientifically knew…

Evolution of man has its spiritual rituals, entanglements with
miscegenation in a bloody human nation chilled with cold human
sensations marked with our nation's national Anthem so shall we stand

to sing the songs of truth of our ancestors for generations to come,
my man?

Denmark Vessey…Sojourner Truth…Ida B. Wells…
John Brown and Nat Turner too were all brave Americans
Who stood for liberation, so we pour libation to remember their names

America, America, land of the free, home of the brave,
never turn your back on our people, the descendants of former slaves,
so its sins can wash away and this great nation can be saved

For I am not the son of Sha Clack Clack!
I am from before that…before before…

America, America…America!

Speculation

They speculate about me
But I know who I am, God lets me call him me!

I'm the screenwriter writing my own personal soliloquies…on
blank acrylic canvases that represent my theoretical,
hypothetical mental scenarios, so what's your scenario

I'm Skit-scatting through life on my musical soundtracks;
complex with syncopated harmonies and intricate melodies
Extroverted and introverted when needed B and reaping what
I sowed…

Representing my grandfather's great great grandfather….
(ya know?)

Don't ask me his name…he was not someone with great fame
because I don't know him He didn't leave me nothing…but
just the slave owner's last name

Jim Crow know 100 years ago there were no black civil rights
or the right to vote

Redlining neighborhoods because of segregation…But see,
Desegregation left black folks without property & promissory
notes and just blank checks

We once had black dentists and doctors and inventors

Not just pro-athletes and rappers at concerts waiting on
microphone checks

So let's not speculate anymore about me.
Let ME define me and my black multicultural reality.

If black lives really mattered in our community we wouldn't
harm each other, ya see I'm just a writer speaking heart to
heart through my poetry.

I've got a third eye and a very creative imagination...

So No more speculation

Cried Eyes for 235

I've got cried criticized Eyes for 235...
The negrito people of Ecuador are prideful people...living in
brick huts...inside the Andes Mountains, alone in them huts
minus the mestizos from la encomienda

Brick huts tucked with African Ecuadorians

Huts made from hands tucked away deep within the Andes
Mountains, where the homegrown nuts that sing humdrums and
fun-filled situations and they know about Trump...beans and rice
to serve...the privileged people who come to visit...beans grown
in the earth that are made to eat...the elderly had no shoes on
her feet but her spirit You nor anyone could defeat...

235 kilometers from Quito

El Capital...no, no tour bus can reach the people...of 235.
Walk and climb into their village and you must take the same
route coming out...

They say Mama Alicia...Mama Alicia, Bienbenidos, Mama
Alicia.

Are You surprised that I have serious cried eyes for village
235??

55 Shots

55 gun shots made the city blocks hot.
Why shoot ya shot during corona? The invisible virus?

Ain't people dying proof for ya?

Grandma, grandpa…and uncles…are afraid

No need for them 55 gunshots to blaze

Why make the city blocks hot during again the worst
healthcare crisis of age?

Influenza…like didn't ya think somebody could get hurt?

Can't you see another way to win?

The coronavirus

It's a global pandemic…

Yeah, the block been hot while our black & brown been
slinging them amethyst rocks. It's a way out of poverty

Like give me a fix of that purple rain that drives brains insane
in the membranes…

55 gunshots made my city blocks hot…let's represent peace.
Why not?

Urban Kings

Urban Kings are kings that earn respect for things that are not given in concrete jungles

Kings want the big-concept things who can flash, then take things from others but don't and won't because of street codes that knows somebody's got a loaded fo-fo

His timeclock says he can move throughout the urban blocks but not be clocked by another brother but feared because his hands skills are real ill and everybody knows that. He comes from that boom bap…but boom seems to loom in dark nights where hand-to-hand combat and fights ain't right no more but blue steel still dominates the heartbeats like break beats in many beatdowns and defeats in urban settings with shells that smell like hot gun powder. Like power that corrupts and hides the mind from greatness and success.

But who truly can pass that urban street test?

Don't test me, b…because I simply be that guy who wants to survive these mean streets, you see…

I need a future so I can meet my future daughters… They want to be able to call me Daddy.

I want longevity, can't you see? Street things are made for these when you witness police brutality. George Floyd can't breathe. King.

Street things are made of these things, urban kings, so many losses…but everybody can't be a boss. So what can you gain and at what cost?

Truth

Truth be told, once you turn old with family secrets,

Secrets are to behold for a lifetime

Truth be told, those secrets can cause a lifetime full of great pain.

That pain is stained in the membrane forever.

Truth be told, it is taboo for you to tell the truth

So keep them family secrets a secret and you will be seen

As normal.

Truth be told, no one is normal. Those are all lies.

Cried eyes come from lies crushed and suppressed by other lies.

Truth be told, once the elders become old and those stories are eventually told…

They live on through generations of old. Learn your lessons so the bad truth gets old so

those things do not repeat themselves and happen again.
Those feelings and emotions are carried on into relationships with others. Especially if and when the secrets are shared by the mothers…

Truth be told, over and over and over. Again. But regardless, you must fight to win!

Baby Black Boy

Baby black boy, you will grow to enormous size and strengths.

Your innocence will be tainted because of your color and your curled hair and your beautiful dark brown eyes...and melanated skin

So dig the skin you're in and win

Baby black boy, you didn't choose who you are or what you are...The heavens did that on purpose...

Baby black boy, don't worry

Your joy will come from your purpose and your passion.

Keep your eyes on the prize and listen to the music and rhythms of life

Be happy...find joy along the journey

Because all the hate for you is just unfiltered noise.

Baby black boy, you will grow to enormous size and strength... so celebrate the great legacy of your ancestors

Don't worry about fame...simply serve others in some sorta way

Baby black boy, people shall remember your name

People shall remember your name...

People SHALL remember your...

Name...

You are my baby black boy...because I am your father.

Realize

Realize that I was born with them bright eyes and hopes and dreams to pursue; that had to be realized and capitalized without being monetized

Realize them dreams had to come to fruition by you and only you.

But that college Tuition got me in debt too.

So I remember sitting in the philosophy classes studying premises and fallacies

And reading fifty pages at night, not retaining my reasoning for being in debt for my future.

Once you realize that debt is all on you, you must create a way to pay and fix up your financial literacy skills because it's all about that credit. Yeah, I said it.

It is time to monetize your creativity and fix your credit.

Realize

Not Done
(Inspired by Jay-Z)
Ecuador, July 3, 2017

I'm not done with the work for the world…

I've had great teachers and preachers teach me the golden jewels, so get with me, young…not just in the classroom but in the world…so I teach…so I've got more rooms of lessons for the next group of youth to teach that are consciously aware of truth

Who seeks out truth…

Geometry and Trigonometry took some youth away from their hopes and dreams as entrepreneurs…those movers and shakers and doers…saved from the life of executive consecutive corporate slave plantations…because they didn't know the calculus but…14 moons divide themselves in cycles of 23… Michael was genius at what he do or did at 23 with 23 on his chest and he's still the best that ever played the game

Do not worry about the riches and fame…focus on the game you play…be the best at that game which you've chosen to play and break night until the light of day…

Runnin', Runnin'…Running away from your true destiny…too focused on who else won… when I know you…him…her and I are the chosen ones…

Still seeking…'cause I'm simply NOT done!

Hear the Silence

I hope I hear the silence for once
Take me away from the New York hustle
Because I need me to reflect upon me
And where do I wanna be in five years and in ten years in the
near future…

My future is intertwined with your future
A future that has promise
A future that has hopes and dreams to pursue…
Which may be predicted upon how u react to the fiscal
responsibilities I wanna pursue

Why be impulsive…
Why jump at every opportunity that costs money…

Try saving some for later…in case of an emergency…

New clothes and fancy cars are conspicuously purchased by me
and you!

Wanna Be...

I wanna be a man focused on the important things...

I wanna be a living, breathing man holistically...

One who understands the world and thinks globally and spiritually...

I wanna be who I was simply intended to be...before I knew I was actually me...

And intellectually...I want to learn eternally

My learning should leave noble deeds that leave an imprint upon my lineage and Legacy

If one man could change the world...I'd hope he could be me...

Significantly...

CLICK-CLICK

CLICK-CLICK…GO AHEAD AND TAKE YOUR PIC

Colors…compositions…and content are important elements

Love for the beauty and for the humanities…

So come with me and capture my love, sweet lady…
kiss the full lips.

Click-click…flash-flash.

I like seeing you excited about seeing me…Even without
the cash.

CLICK-CLICK

That strong energy is positive energy for me…receive me…

I've come so far…

Reza

Erecta

Click-CLICK went the lights…

Feel and touch…in the darkness…with clear vision and no sight.

Click-Click, I say…

Because I am NOT the son of ShaClack Clack…I am from
before that…I am before before…

Click-Click

Connection

Connect with me

Connect with me

Bring forth your positive energy

Energy is translucent and free

It don't cost you nothing

Except your thoughts and pure synergy...

Think of the beauty of nature's colorful tapestry and the creativity within our own humanity and you'll see positive things discovered and explored throughout time's human curiosity for centuries to come.

Connect with me

Because I can feel YOUR energy

By simply seeing you and you seeing me...

Humans connecting with other humans can be beautiful regardless of skin color or religion or political party affiliations...

Connect with me even if we disagree, verbally.

Home

What if I created a home full of fun

And joyful occasions

Playful activities…that create warm laughter and hardy giggles…

What if I created a home that was free from anger and drama and conflict

What if I created a pleasant home I could enjoy coming home to to escape the busy world

A home I could call by phone that's my own.

A home for a beautiful wife and family

What if I had a home to create my own magic; filled with a beautiful clean tapestry that had a beautiful aroma. (Hummm)

A home filled with musical symphonies composed by Steven Sondheim and Quincy Jones…

Home, you see, could be my escape from the cold cold world…

Abandoned

We messed up now…

Where Daddy at?

He left? Why?

Oh, no, we all messed up now!

I need him, Mama.

What are we supposed to do now?

How we gonna get food to eat?

What he say…

Call Aunt Mae

How am I supposed to live to see another day?

I need Daddy.

I know I think I'm grown but did he leave anything for me?

Land, or investment properties?

I wanted to attend the university.

No? Nothing? But I am only just 18! I'm about to turn 19.

Homeless.

We Raise Our Hands

(Dedicated to the Youth of America who used their voices to
end gun violence in our schools)

We raise our hands to stop gun violence in our schools

And use our common sense without pistols and assault rifles
for school defense...

We raise our hands to answer the call for life and everlasting life
for our students and teachers and administrators and faculty
across our beautiful country...

We raise our hands for equality and safety

So don't arm our teachers with guns

Arm our teachers with pens and pencils and computer
technology so that students can better comprehend
mathematics and history and biology...

We raise our hands to educate and support our youth

We raise our hands

We raise our hands

Silence against gun violence makes you compliant toward gun
violence, which makes no sense when young people are dying.

We raise our hands

We raise our hands

We

Raise

Our

Hands with you!

Teen Dreams

Remember when we were teens, we had big dreams?

My teen dreams were very special to me

My imagination had endless possibilities

Music in the 80s and 90s were soundtracks of my hopes and reality

My teen dreams were woven into the American dreams...

Love...joy and a happy life.

I dreamt of finding the most perfect wife

Much of my teen life wasn't filled with political rhetoric and who I am in my cultural American life

Them teen dreams seem to escape me as I make monetary plans and policies for my future playbook on life and age can cut life like a Ginsu knife.

Them teen dreams seem to swiftly pass

So they become lifelong memories from one's oh daunting past...as the crows clock tick and tock but no tick-tock clock can tick tock me.

Those teen dreams make me happy; in fact, very happy, you see.

Human Sensitivity

Sensitive because we raise our hands

Sensitive because I'm among the living and my heart still beats...with human blood through human veins and human wide feet

Heartbeats are like hip-hop break beats that recycle with the timing that's anticipated

So just talk to me so you can see what's my reality...race, class and ethnicity coexist in urban cities...but what about the countryside near the tumbleweeds silent from street cars and distracting sounds...within those rural towns...colonial homes with exclusivities

What's going on, my people...can't u all see

Who's the target of human brutality

Let's find our common humanity

Father, we don't need to escalate

War is not the answer, for only love can conquer hate

Otherwise Poverty can't continue to escalate

RACE for the Stars

Probably Caucasian…

Probably African…

The Afro-Centric Asian!

Half man. Half Amazing…

You may think you're one…

But you are many…

The confluence of them all…

No matter how wide

No matter how tall or strong.

Probably simply human…

Probably…Oh!

He or she…is probably mulatto.

Race for the stars no matter who you are…

John Singleton…51…

Boyz in Ya Hood…Heaven

Bring Me Back

Please bring me back to land my ancestors once knew…

I want to see them blue skies and bright yellow and black butterflies…too

Please bring me back to a place far, far, far away

They call it the motherland

So I can simply say…I walked on the land that my ancestors once knew.

I touched the soils of eternity. My feet shall sink in the sands of the Sahara

Because beyond eternity is ONLY eternity

Because I am who I am…I am from before.

Before before…Before they built the pyramids when dawns were still young.

But will they the natives see me as strange fruit?

Will they witness the melanin deep within my skin that displays my ancestral roots??

The hardworking sons of slaves with no work boots…and tattered sores on their feet…but he don't know defeat…even during slavery…shucking corn or picking cotton.

African diaspora.

Nippsey
(A dedication to life & legacy of Nippsey Hustle)

If a man…why not a black man…

If a man can…why not a black man can..?

Who is he in human history?

Is he the darkness of night that stole the human light from
humanity?

Robbing…Stealing, Gang Banging or Selling rocks on nectars,
block slinging amethyst rocks?

Or

Is he the light that shines in dark nights that represents life and
the beautiful children of the night?

If a man…who is the TRUE black man?

Is he like Superman?

Is he Faster than speeding light? Is he faster than a bullet from
other black brothers? Does black lives really matter? Is he More
powerful than a locomotive!

Is the black man Able to leap tall buildings in a single bound?

Is he SuperNegro?

Yes, Yes, it's SuperNegro...strange visitor from another planet, who came to Earth with powers and abilities far beyond those of mortal men.

SuperNegro, who can change the course of mighty rivers, bend steel with his bare hands, and who is disguised as the Sandman...Clark Kent, the candy man who can dance! Mr. Bojangles! He can tap dance! His rhythmic motion can move to the rhythms of humdrums...can you see the wind blow through the urban trees and the concrete?

He is sometimes a mild-mannered man and sometimes an angry man because of oppression and poverty...for he fights a never-ending battle for truth, justice like no other man can... stop, I can't breathe...please, I can't breathe and it's the American way.

If no other man can...SuperNegro certainly can!!! Look up... it's a bird...It's a plane...no, it's Superman!

Shout out to Nippsey...now go Hustle!!!

Elevate

Elevate & concentrate on the things that really matter.

What matters is that you listen to the heartbeats and break beats…and find out what's calling you to do things that allow you to create and go gold as you grow older

Innovate, elevate and create something that's never been created before

Blaze your own trail

Then find your truth

Realize it's time to self-actualize

Elevate.

Evicted

I cut through grass and blaze new paths for others to follow…I stand tall on the shoulders of ancestors that came before us whose spirits follow us as I stand firm on hollow grounds…and platforms unfound…

Do you hear the sounds of achievements echoing through the trees as the wind-blown spirits whisper the truth?

The next generational success is in the hands of our youth… don't shoot the children, I shout… don't shoot the children… for they are already infected with complex time and shine and how to shine and when to shine and it's my time to shine in their mindset…

Let's reset their mindset…for their future…microphone check, microphone checka…

Riggady Bow!!! What's gonna happen now…our water's contaminated…there's a recall on Walmart's fruit…and lead paint on radiators are poisonous…too…so don't shoot! Stealing our mind was the greatest thing you thought you did…fortunately I mastered the matrix as a kid…so I could clearly see what you did…

Therefore I cut through grass and blaze new paths for others to follow…

It's the department of defense…

Buck Bennie told me to tare down the fence…and be a trail blazer.

Stand Tall

We shall stand tall and proud…

Because we made them pyramids when dawns were young so respect the geometrical formula

Life's journey shall come with some surprises and fun

We shall stand tall and proud during tough times too because it's the life lessons that either make or break you

Transform you into new dimensions

Frcsh…anew

Whatever is not growing is dead

Life is forever eternal

Ask our maternal ancestors who came before us

Thus in the name of Fannie Lou Hammer, Tubman, Ida B., Nikki G., Parks, and countless others.

And the countless unnamed.

We shall stand without fame.

MLK Day (Speech)
Mount Carmel Church
January 21, 2020

Emerson once said...God speaks to us through our imagination...King said I have a Dream...so pay attention to God...and his unchanging hands...and imagine a world where equality and justice for all prevailed...

So use your Imagination and create...and go gold...

The Rev Dr. Martin Luther King's legacy continues to live on through us...

We are all men & women, Christians of Noble deeds...

King would say today...We must unite regardless of our differences...now more than ever before...We must serve those who are poverty stricken...those who have no voice.

So Elevate & concentrate on the things that matter.

What matters is that you listen to the true heartbeats and break beats...in our community and find out what's calling you to do things that allow you to create and go gold as we grow together...

Innovate...elevate and create something that's never been created before for humanity.

Blaze your own trail.

Then find your truth.

Realize it's time to self-actualize.

Imagine the power we possess collectively...United as one...

If They Knew (Me)

If they only knew about the young boy who was drowning in the pool in Pennsylvania and I saved him from the waters of that wave pool...

If they only knew I witness God through the Wind-Blown spirits and the old bones & shells too

If they only knew my step-daddy was my real daddy and he didn't have his father's surname too...

If they only knew Harriet said, "if they only knew they were slaves, then she would have freed more slaves, if they only knew...

If they only knew that little girl and her mother on West End Avenue whose car flipped over and I ran to their rescue and my college friends at Morehouse didn't know what to do.

If they only knew.

If they only knew in Chicago I had the flu and ended up in a free clinic for help with no health insurance with that damn flu.

If they only knew a Mexican man was having a heart attack and nobody in that ER Room big like a gymnasium spoke Spanish except me with my sickened influenza.

The nurse and doctors didn't know his native tongue but I knew…

I helped save his life through my translations too. "Senor, donde esta su Delor? En su cabesa y en su abrazo, y tu tienes mucho delor en su carazon tambien?" Nurse he's having a heart attack…cardiac arrest!

That's only a few situations that God used me to help someone else during my life journey too.

So you shouldn't criticize me; I wish you only knew.

What's Next

Okay, you say the truth about the injustices on a group of our people

You say the God's-honest truth about decades of abuse we know about Jim Crow up from the days of ancestor roots hanging from a noose, but what's next?

Where do we go from there? How do we dispel great fears of the past so that I might live a better now…'cause time's beating our ass…and how do we fast track our ambitions to God's unknowing past?

Where do we go from here to there, where I wanna be…ya see, we got popular music and rhythmic beats…high hats that make us recite rhymes and rhythmic beats and lyrics and catch lines standing in bread lines for food…oh, Corona…or sitting in our seats…at a Ludacris concert…

Ya see, we got Beyoncé & Jay-Z. Billionaires in black to see

P. Diddy and Andre and Heavy D, uptown's now kickin it, poppin' bottles and shining bling-bling. Mr. Champagne, take your seat and do your thing

We took the front lines of our pride and let the world see our shine in music videos

But where do we go from here, I say…

Where do we go from here, I say...

Do we simply say ASHE? And be done?

The Message

Message for today: Black people including myself...have NEVER been a monolithic people! We are all different! We are VERY diverse!! We all play different roles in our fight for justice & equality for America! We cannot afford to criticize one another for what and how we process the tragedy we are currently experiencing, along with the tragedy that has existed for centuries...

We must be sensitive toward each other and to others outside of our culture who too recognize the pain. Change is gonna come. But in that process we cannot verbally abuse each other as we proceed to heal and grow.

We all may have a very different method in achieving the same goal. But again, let's work hard at creating solutions to a very big problem that has existed for centuries in this great nation and around the world.

Every man in his day plays a different part in reconciliation. Violence & Destruction must take a back seat in this...Peace and Equality...and JUSTICE must prevail now...

The message has been made loud and clear.

So let's plan...plot...organize and mobilize that important change strategically.

Only light can eliminate the darkness...

In love,

Mr. Mayor

Who Shall Stand
(A poem dedicated to the man that never married
my mom...he's my dad, Woolah)

Who shall stand for this man?

Who shall stand for this man like he stood for you before you
knew you...

Who shall stand, I say?

Today. Tomorrow and yesterday...

Who shall stand for this man; his time has expired so who did
HE inspire?

Who shall stand, I say...As we stand to represent a man of
noble deeds.

His transition to the other side has been seen as very weary and
weak

88 is the age and date to this date

Who's paid the great dues for his inspiration ?

Only if you knew his human history filled with actions that
solidify his legacy...embedded within me and your legacy...

His mom and father may have dealt with his birth as a tragedy,

So Who…shall…stand for…this MAN?

PeNManShip

My penmanship represents the writings of my life's journey...
it self-populates and creates a lane for my vision to shine and
summarize neurological transmissions in the brain that
stimulates electrical impulses of bad memories of the pain that
makes ME insane in the membrane and all the good times and
the bad times that create the rough, tough edges carved into
my character...ill met by the moonlight, she said...

But my penmanship equates rhymes with reason, the times
with seasons...through the hills and the valleys...the curves
and crooked lines of my joy and pain...like the sunshine and
the rain...my trials and tribulations...But don't shoot the
children, I shout. Don't shoot the children!!! Because they
need more time...they need more time, time to finish their
journey...

Who's privy to the inside stories?

How do I write the songs on my legacy for generations to
come..? Does legacy align with four-part harmonies? Music
soothes the savage beast...and yes and yes and yes, the lions in
the mighty jungles might sleep tonight...shhh...silence so we
can hear wind and the sounds of the mighty seas. Can you hear
the wind-blown spirits blow through the tall green trees?

But where did the writings begin?

How can I say that I've walked among the greatest of men within my penmanship of old...

Use YOUR elements to be great and go gold.

Decipher my penmanship and then translate it to Peter before I get to them pearly gates...and to the future generations, no never need for hate...you're too great!...and to the generations of old!

Again! My penmanship represents me... (Pause) & my true legacy!

Know Your Passion & Purpose (Speech)

November 3, 2019
Springfield Baptist Church (Beacon, New York)

Know Your Position and Play Your Position
in the Covenant of God

My culture stems from the beginning Time in human history...
so pour the libation in the Atlantic and praise God for the birth
and fossil resurrection of Lucy...the oldest human fossils found
in Olduvai Gorge, Mother Africa

Shout out the archeological digs of Mary and Lewis B.
Leakey and the significant sounds of natural resources extracted
from that land for obstructionist consumption capitalist
worldwide and to all the hell he send thee...

And finally, my culture stems from a bloody untold human
history that too captures the hidden colors of forever...

Colors of colorful rainbow as thirteen moons divide themselves
in cycles of twenty-three. Holy father, Holy grail, sing praises for
the holy trinity...study up, black boys, and learn the journey of
human history...Ghana...Songhai and Kingdoms of Mali

Wrap this knowledge around your consciousness and dig the
skin you're in...

How you count your days and time shall define or confine or
hide the mind from greatness...it's time to watch your sunrise
and shine...

My culture stems from the beginning of...TIME!

Greetings...to Pastor Dr. Perry, the First Lady, Clergy, other
dignitaries, Deacons and family & friends of the Springfield

Baptist Church. Giving honor to God and to my Lord and Savior Jesus Christ, who is first in my life...I've come with greetings and a brief yet profound message today all the way from Newburgh, NY...and my message is entitled "Position and Power"...and church, repeat after me...tell your neighbor to KNOW your position...PLAY your position and KNOW the power of God... if you know the power of God...you will soon know your assignment that he has given you for the glory of the kingdom of God in heaven...

Now see, before you can know your assignments and before you know your position...and before you can play your position in life...you must FIRST know and discover WHO you are... then you have to know WHOSE you are...

Now now knowing who you are comes within time and a series of events and trials and tribulations and failures and a battery of tests. These tests may even bring you close to death... These tests are God's way of knowing who you are and whose you are in the grand scheme of things according to HIS will...in the good book Job was tested in this regard...the old song writer said you'll understand it better by-and-by.

So once again know your position...play your position and understand the power of God...

In the book of Jeremiah 29:11 it states...for I know the plans I have for you, declares the Lord... plans to prosper you and not to harm you...plans to give you hope and a future...

The Bible also says in the 23rd Psalms

¹ The Lord is my shepherd; I shall not want.

² He maketh me to lie down in green pastures: he leadeth me beside the still waters.

³ He restoreth my soul: he leadeth me in the paths of
righteousness for his name's sake.

⁴ Yea, though I walk through the valley of the shadow
of death, I will fear no evil: for thou art with me;
thy rod and thy staff they comfort me.

⁵ Thou preparest a table before me in the presence of
WHO???…mine enemies: thou anoints my head
with oil; my cup runneth over.

⁶ Surely GOODNESS and MERCY shall follow me
ALL the days of my life: and I will dwell in the
house of the Lord for ever and ever and ever…

So I decided to step outside of my comfort and convenience
as a History Teacher and run in 2015 for City Council at large
and won. Then 2 1/2 years on the City Council our then Mayor
was reassigned to the heavens and earned her wings after a long
battle with a private medical illness…she ordered me to her
bedside seven days before her passing…her number-one wish
was that I complete her term as Mayor…then I was appointed
Mayor shortly after with a unanimous vote by the city council…
Then three weeks later our city was hit with a Tornado!! Our
city manager and department heads and I responded
immediately…we mobilized the Red Cross…Salvation Army
and fifty electric trucks to go from 97% of our residents without
power, including our elderly and senior community…to 100%
fully restored power in just THREE days!! We were tested. I
had to pray silently…The only fatality we had was a 9-year-old
girl who died in her mom's car by a falling tree which crushed
her as her mom was taking groceries into the house during the
storm…we had to comfort the mother and family…outside of

that act of nature. Our command center pulled off miracles during the storm…residents and restaurant owners even went out to the streets and did pop-up barbecues to feed our community in four different neighborhoods…and I've been on my assignment as Mayor ever since…I won a special election last November to complete the former Mayor's term. Now I'm currently serving a full four years term…since being re-elected. We have since appropriated $4 million or more for new roads and ADA-compliant sidewalks and curbs… We've sold over $1 million dollars worth of city owed properties that were on our vacancy list in one year.

We've partnered with a fews major developers and the State Land bank and Habitat For Humanity to fix up and restore more than 15 abandoned buildings in our city into a 15 million-dollar project to create 45 more new apartments for low-income housing…and just two homicides in our city for the year 2018. …but during our budget season in 2018 our then City Manager…put in a resignation…the comptroller…did so too… our Director for city planning and economic development… recently resigned as well…we have since hired a new city manager and a new comptroller and a new director of planning and economic development who are young and very competent. We also have the Mayor's Economic & Development Advisory Committee who are finalizing three development projects as we speak…Our city is revitalizing with a strategic plan! These solutions are in place already…but…because of faith and because I know who I am and whose I am…I know my position…I am playing my position and I fully know the power of God!!! Prayer works, y'all…I've been charged to complete my assignment serving others…No matter what storms come and go…we have and ALL will be tested!! But when you know the source that sits up high...but looks down low...you understand the covenants of God! When God is for ya...who can be against ya!

So I conclude by saying...that you have a Pastor in charge who's been given his assignment right here in this beautiful church with a path that leads to truth and righteousness!!

Pastor Perry is already in position...Mayor Torrance Harvey is already in position...continue to pray for me...continue to pray for the Pastor and his strength in the Lord and speak to the heavens directly for your assignment in assisting him...stay on the path...keep the faith, Springfield...

Dr. King once said...

"Everybody can be great...because anybody can serve. You don't have to have a college degree to serve. You don't have to make your subject and verb agree to serve. You only need a heart full of grace. A soul generated by love."

Thank you, Springfield, for your invite today. Thank you, Pastor Perry, and your family and the church for having me... my visit here in Beacon is a blessing!!! I hope to return very soon! May God keep you...all.

Know your position...and play your position and know the power of God...God's assignment is waiting for you!! Now serve...

And remember...be nice to somebody somewhere...and somebody somewhere will be nice to you...why?

Because it's just nice to be nice!!

Amen

Reflection

When I awake in the morning…All I see in the truthful mirror
is me…

The me that wonders how the world sees me as my life's
history is being recorded upon the annals of history…

How will others from generations to come reflect upon me and
the things that I have done..!? Or the New things they may see
within me that I in my lifetime didn't see…

Who is the real me..?

What is my true reality?

Did I ever reach my destiny?

Throughout life I hope to share and enlighten

while being enlightened…I hope to leave my

handprint on the world so someone

somewhere can say there was a man of Noble

Deeds…one who had the passion and courage

to try when others dared not try…humility and

human compassion for others are the greatest

gifts given to me by people of great influence

and therefore I extend that to all I come in

contact with while on my special journey...

So write me a memorandum with the promises of human prosperity

Clean air, Clean water and study war no more.

Life's most persistent and urgent question is "What are we doing for others?"

RUN

Run like your life depends on it.

Run like no other has ever run like you before

Or done it like you done it so run

Chase your dreams for they are your dreams to dream.

Paint your picture and picture your success on blank canvasses with what your imagination runs with for eternity.

Run like your eternity is tied to your destiny and what you see and believe you to see.

Run! Just Run!

CPSIA information can be obtained
at www.ICGtesting.com
Printed in the USA
JSHW021539290821
18219JS00001B/6